A DEEPER
Contemplation

Perry Douglas Sisk

Recall the Spirit

How do we as individuals escape our
memories of our past
those that are good and precious
we cling to tho yet those we hope will last
In each of our lives we've lived some prosper
through the years
though times in deep despair
we gather up our tears
Those roads we chose to travel
with paths off here and there
always seeking others
we'd hope would share our care
Should God see me ever worthy
to earn a set of wings
to carry my spirit across an ocean of time
to hear where an angel sings
When men dream dreams and ponder visions given
will there still be time to earn his grace
this life had always driven
So strive to seek redemption and
attone for errors made
throughout our lives to seek
that tree of life and shelter in its shade

Forgive us oh lord for making
all the wrong choices and
going down all the wrong roads
A life we had led that kept us from seeing
you carried my burdens load
Forsake us not oh father now that time is nigh
this we now know better to walk with
your spirit to carry us on so high
That instant we take that final breath
of this life and exhale into the next

Those mighty words of God found in only
one book with all its text
This bible holds one passage from here
to eternity
A life that's everlasting once recalled the spirit
I see reflections of heaven's stars
upon the seas and hope to
be drawn near it

Perry Douglas Sisk

Free Will I Sing

May 7, 2023

Reflections of the skies on waters
reveal elusive dreams
inspired unto our sons and daughters
a love so hoped for seems
Profound their care so sought for there
so seldom ever found
in time to spare those feelings
swear to never voice a sound
What fondness do we feel for
what is otherwise real
is what we cannot workaround
things that take us back
a song a fragrance a dream we remember
a coin we once had found

Oh, so simple it all seems to be
those issues coming to
mind for you and me
All the beauty of this world
we look past every day
one answer to one question
never will we see or say
Gone unnoticed through decades
into century long
The glory and the praise
to God simply voiced in a song
Free will being right
never seeing what was wrong

Perry Douglas Sisk

A TREASURED UPBRINGING

May 3, 2023

Those who practice what they preach
are all too often guided to one day teach
Far too many left to reach
those grains of sand on a beach
Those stars at night we try to count
though doing so in vain
Knowing all too well there never will be
a measured number to gain
Folks long past who used to cast
their cautions to the wind
were so permitted to follow their dreams
to see just where they end
A penny found on the ground
its face side pointed up
is said to offer luck to some
yet never fills their cup
As a kid one thing I did
was fish along a creek
one baited hook was all it took
to find some sport I'd seek
Those days back then outdoors we'd spend
with idle times we had
even chores left more to find
those thoughts both good and bad
My grandma would preach what school would not teach
those things all kids should learn
always give respect to elders
or be whooped from stem to stern
One thing can be said of the older class
their methods thought so bold
doing right by those who fight not
to be seen as cold
For now by full measure being raised with traits

A Deeper Contemplation

so seldom seen
those lessons taught they thought for naught
a treasure thought lost and yet
not bought my upbringing a treasure
given free

Perry Douglas Sisk

Fear To Shed

May 19, 2023

Where again do we begin
each new day we dare not offend
Within each rising sun
that casts its warmth abroad
to invent a newer concept
that some will deem as flawd
Are we all placed into this world
with no clear path to follow
with each new day emotions sway
in truth one bitter pill to swallow
These later days we now do say
those years they passed so fast
and left to wonder just more
to ponder just who will who outlast
With heavy sigh one grasp of an eye
that turns away its view
for fear of knowing corruption some
were sewing the truth in lies they knew
Has it not been so that those we know
were ones that come and go
Falling to the rear
of those that fear
the eye that shed one tear

A Heart Apart

May 21, 2023

I feel that most will fail to
admit they will one day reach a stage
where nothing much will matter anymore
being less impressed by age
Giving way to dreams of a heart
so willing to be revealed
those hidden desires to be more than we are
as secrets kept so sealed
If given a glimpse of a future foretold
as a history did so tell
That knowledge and wisdom once was gained
that failed to fill a well
Those so blind though eyes that see
do always fully deny
Many who claim to be wise will repeat
their folly and be the ones that cry
Haughty in nature with arrogant ways
does always stand apart
those seen as opposing a majority rule
are the class of the purer heart

Perry Douglas Sisk

Not So Lost At All

June 8, 2023

My take on what life accounts for
as being a book yet written
holding many chapters and many pages
all to reflect for whom we once were smitten .
All the things both small and large
a life dissected is made of
what keeps it together or sets
life apart is always for sake of love
A life that hides in guilt or shame for having
done or failed for reason never brought to light
This struggle in ones self gone on
through years concealed ones inner fight
Why some will always strive to elude
a fate so destined for
As fishermen cast their nets to harvest
before they reach the shore

Another day of hoped for inspirations
from where we know not it falls
As a sparrow God gave its flight both by day
and even night its mate it hopes it calls
All those that i knew
having gone before me
Still living well entrusted to
our hearts and memory
One day soon we too will
once again join along and beside
those hearts those loved ones
in eternity to always abide
so none were lost at all

Does God Rewind Our Time

April 7, 2023

Why does it appear so foreign
to this younger class today
there still are people among us too
so unwilling to obey
Recalling back on sixty years or so
when TV was black and white
A generation left behind in minds of youth
so fearful of the light
A light that brings to forefront
those so held by thoughts of then
with hopes and dreams of better times
that share this wish to win
All the things well hidden behind a veil
of darker intent kept sealed
Those held to truth that clear a path
for those their eyes revealed
History it seems to always repeat
as is what's been noted today
unrest and persecutions that seem
resurrected from a
time known not so far away
As planets around our Sun do follow
their orbits so stable by design
As humanity has followed the
Son of God a true analogy we find
For all these times
within his lines
a time that God rewinds

Perry Douglas Sisk

One Task God Gave His Son
EASTER 2023
(Contemplate This)

Say we lived in a world where every
object speaks, plants and animals,
and even trees conversed with
voices meek
To stretch our imaginations more
the lions voice in baritone
to amplify his roar
while smaller creatures in lesser tone
the shriek as eagles soar
This world created by design
our father holds full domain
while seasons pass with timely manner
in each does fall the rain
The mind of man with gifted reason
knows not discernment of
why our hearts lean to compassion
for all things there is LOVE
Some become immune to what
others see as empathy
becoming numb to sensitivity for others
that may still share some sympathy
A heart that no longer feels compassion for another
Has been told of long before
as one brother admonished the other
what more was left in store
Why a people so much alike
their hair, their limbs One heart
encased in varied color of skin
Never being meant to be
oh so set part
This one gift given that
all do share this common thread we keep

This blood that flows throughout our veins
with eyes that always weep
One shepherd high above
protecting all his sheep
This one solid symbol keeping all people one
Red is the Blood that Jesus shed
with that his task was done

Revealed In Truth

April 9, 2023

Do many question why
we were brought into this life
that we are forced to evolve
and grow along with bitter strife
If we all would hold to truth
that our beings were absent of reason
failing to repel the lies
some depict as outright treason
Closely captured and grouped together but
solely isolated in our own transparent nature
Some will lack the sight for what
they see to fight while others
hide in darkness with fear of cleansing light
For light was meant for all to see the
fear that kept us enslaved and so alone
The absence of what dare not be shown
this light of truth with chance atone
Inside of this will all be free
no longer hidden or obscured
that cloak of deception those
blind was once so lured
into that abyss where light
never shines
within my faith this light
my soul will find
It is all revealed in truth

An Angel On My Cheek

April 12, 2023

Are there truly angels that
assuredly walk where mortals rarely see
Giving guidance when all else fails
for who we're caused to be
Those twists and turns this life's
path yearns for straighter directions take
Is it an angel that whispers softly
on what course not to make
Shadows hide what we know inside
to always be mindful of
Hope and pray stay the light of the day
when push will come to shove
When danger nears that build our fears
Two voices do we hear
One to our left and other to our right
an angel makes it clear
We know its been said
only the good die young
but do they really pass
Those that parted far too soon
hand-picked for angels class

So yes I feel that they are real
those subtle signs we miss
a voice we hear a sudden tear
did feel an angel's kiss

Perry Douglas Sisk

Thought To Deep To Share

April 11, 2023

So as it turns out my being the
unlikely one who always had possessed
Something held for many years
kept deep within and oh so well been hidden
Little was i ever aware that one day would come a test
To pick or choose what some would loose
or hope was not forbidden

All this while in glorified style
that some looked on as taken
aback was i when cast aside
in youth was deemed forsaken
Lacking too any vision through
these years would soon reveal
This gift lay dormant behind those
shadows that come to light and feel
A depth of seeing through his maze
of tangled thoughts not voiced
As one door closes does another really
open I did so have a choice
Open wide that gate that show a fate
I did so hold myself
call it gifted or a soul that shifted
sharing dreams placed on my shelf

INSIGHT TO VISION

April 12, 2023

Have there not been times throughout
mans history Dividing times Uniting times
within these lines we see
One goal so fought for though
seen as diminished by greater powers be
allow for being finished
Time and time again those that
fell upon their swords, never doing so
in vain touting honor for their lords

Fatal images brought to light
for a devastation of
those lives they'd hoped would
once revive for sakes of all their love
So solid this conviction with facets
of complete resolve
No better found or find a way
they hope they could evolve
Call it looking back to a
time I was not in
with visioned indignations
for a multitude of sin
A price we pay and some will say
was brought upon ourselves
So few those battles ever won
be they numbered ten or twelve

An image in a mirror
just may allow a better look
One picture speaks without those
words never written in a book
That often stated adage
that a man's revenge will seek a justice never seen

Perry Douglas Sisk

for what its worth a mountains highest peak
one final judgment call leaves no one left to speak
Where we went and where we've been
So scribed in bolder text
History does replay itself
why ask ourselves what's next

A Proven Cure

April 14, 2023

Looking out my windows view
one early morning of spring
I saw a dove that once
did sing that hallowed lonesome coo

There not too far across my yard
two squirrels sat chewing nuts that fell
From this tree high on a branch
sat cardinals chirping lots to tell

I often note this stillness of
a peace this picture hides
while somber at times as breezes blow
away what nature provides

Those waters of a nearby stream
with sounds so pure and clean
does calm ones soul and puts
to ease to know just where to lean

All these things that lift our hearts
and minds to observe all things so pure
For all our self-inflicted wounds
our spirits feel
within is found a cure

Perry Douglas Sisk

Why a Child Shall Lead

April 3, 2023

This day I was awakened by a
whisper in my ear, arise and shine and offer
thanks for this day and do not fear

If I could lend a voice which
could travel cross the land, not stopping
at the shores or stalled at desert sands,
I would ask to every nation all those
with sense to hear, were we told as children
that in those mansions way on high not
one will shed one tear,
There will be no sorrow or even strife once
ushered in this everlasting life

For this I know a promise kept
so written in a book, not one single eye that
wept refused to even look,
Should I be granted just one wish
I dare to ever tell, that every soul
upon this world recapture what once was held,
that childhood innocence not to sell

Looked On From Above
March 30, 2023

When I am asked what my plans
are for the day,
I sometimes cut it short
to get along my way
Some will showcase their
character division, while too
there are those as well who
maintain a bold precision
Are there times we have to witness
just who will follow
That watchful eye we all are under
sees our colors too
Those who feel they dare not judge
for fear of much the same
Knowing deep to one day reap
in course of time a flame
Break the heart once
then mend the heart twice
will never ease the pain
just as felt when stood alone this cooling fallen rain
Asking for a rescue from
tormented months and years
giving cause why angels seen
as absent they too are shedding tears
When to raise our voices high
into a sky to ask one single why
Thus we fail to live as one
beneath his watchful eye

Perry Douglas Sisk

A Measured Soul
April 3, 2023

Where has it been said
that excellence resides within a few
For many that calibrate those God-given
traits that no one ever knew
Some will hold a depth of being
that none will ever reach
Still though failing to attain
those lessons yet to teach
Speaking for myself a far greater test
I feel to be at play
A countless measure of our talents
that were left to go astray
How then should our quite deeds
be put on full display
To amaze or profoundly announce
in any given way
This full depiction all too often
so far adversely constrained
For those that hold in lesser degree
abilities so restrained
Held down by chains of
earthly demands might one day
count those numbered grains of sand
An impossible task one and all
may conclude while never placing
limits on what may have this ensued
THIS I PONDER WHAT POWER MORTALS
HOLD WHEN IN FULL REVIEW AND SCOPE
THIS REASON SOME WILL SELL THEIR SOUL
THAN TO HOLD TO FAITH AND HOPE

One Trait To Achieve

April 5, 2023

Never have I felt being
prideful of myself stemming from
being raised to keep those arrogances
high upon a shelf
Those I have known through the
entirety of my life
Hold this similar rearing that expects and knows
to deal with and handle strife
Indeed, I've heard it said ones
Character derived of adversity
as common place as seen of nature
will come a graded nobility

This generation I linger from is
fast becoming lesser known
while time does always run its course
letting go from where it was grown

The older we get the more we have
to look back on with shame or pride of each
nothing being wrong for justly being humble
this greater trail to teach
Never to allow those following behind forget
they too will one day face a mirror
See the time so settled in their
mind with hair now gray and eyes that once were clear

In an ending I would bare this true
conviction Unity can be attained
with shared insight and coalition
to hold combined predictions

Perry Douglas Sisk

Love Within Our Soul

April 5, 2023

When you face your challenges that
come about there always will be those
finding yourself against the wall
no retreat at hand or a path laid forward chose
Only one way out is to look
above in hopes of a ladder
descending down allow to climb to love

Must it always demand the patience of a saint
to tolerate those many discomforts though
in contrast to life itself as seen now growing faint
Have we not so many times asked
what purpose we are given
forced to take this journey on and never
asked we have the drive let alone be driven

Though fragile we are made
as mortal beings be

Should we pass this test on earth
what ending we will see
So great the cause with effects being part of
the one Soul purpose having been given
a chosen one with love

One Seed Of Faith God Planted

May 1, 2023

Here once again I sit alone
though this day out of doors
A morning sun that shines down through
those many clouds that act as shrouds
they too do all ignore
Some will see those born to be
handpicked that stand-alone yet
not so set apart
from that time of conception
give a few that one exception
that follow where the Son resides
in each and every heart
We may have spoken of memories
that linger while never reasoning why
As we question not the Blue
of seas beneath a painted sky
Recall that parable of just one seed
as small a grain of sand
when fed those rays of heaven sun and
rain to make it grow into a tree
that one day shades the land
One spark of faith when panted
where all will one day stand
Side by side this unity shared
increase the love we know who always cared
A Son God gave to part the ways
of Man was so declared
As we hope for true salvation
That Son of God so spared

Perry Douglas Sisk

A Key Of Mind's Eye

April 29, 2023

Shall we look behind the wall of time?
So bold that hides those dreams of old
as yet those crystals chime
Back to days of childhood wonder
fear the darkness crack of thunder
recall those days when some would say
we do give praise to God this day
for being given a chance again
to right the wrongs we missed just when
we felt no one could stay
Growing past that time once tender
disclose what time alone will render
Learn we not that sheltered guidance held
steadfast onto as time progressed
those memories timeless weld
One certainty solid as that rock of ages
dreams so valued more than wages
as some wisdom earned in stages
What keeps some young in heart and
mind that ability to reflect
or simply just rewind
oh so shared in-kind
And to that innocence known
back then though as we aged grew blind
and always failed to see
was kept in minds eye the key

Known Beforehand
April 27, 2023

A sense to reason
that God instilled in men
As I watch a mighty nation
fall from where it once had been
So much obstruction to
what's known as true, turned
right side up for many
but a few
Some no longer bare feelings
of shame for rushing away and turning away
and they dare not tame
Those that just won't learn from
events they were witness to
will always come full circle
for lacking what they knew
Forget and let go
so fine a line to walk
those ears of corn we wait to pick
till stiff becomes its stalk
Thus if we knew then
what now we know
where would lie reason to grow
Those young and those old with far to see
was it all so much oneself
fulfilling simple prophecy

Perry Douglas Sisk

One Kiss Away

April 24, 2023

Some things oh so seldom seen
for lack of just one dream
Folks tho say some
come and go
a light shines bright
grows dim we know
While throughout the years
been heard in song
some written heartbreaks
lasting long dismissed
those flowing tears
Lyrics put to music
with voices echo far
giving cause to name those well
some kept within a jar
Just as canvas sitting blank
within its frame some never
reaching public fame
their passions never sank
All too short a time
do we hold within one life
a cutting edge of change never seen
what practice dulls a knife
This where deep devotion ever true
resides within committed to one's talent
hidden just beneath a fragile skin
strive to catch that far tossed kiss
with still one shallow miss
was still one kiss away
some say

Mother's Heart Acknowledged

April 25, 2023

People travel many highways
their destinations known
keeping steadfast this belief
as roads turn rocky
fear what seeds were sown

Is often said that one good turn
will sure deserve another
fragments of what yet to learn
from our fathers and our mother

Far removed where once we stood
looked back on with some regret
mistaking steps we took for better
judgments come one son does always set
Setting on those lifelong dreams
once held in mind for few it seems
so written in a letter

Knowing all those deeds not done
That speak for just my own
as flowers bloom from seed so sown
we all remain just flesh and bone
leads me now to silent days
where in my home I know
some would view my solitude
would hold how much more to show

To share one's thoughts with varied others
seeking warmth beneath what covers
one hidden need to partthe ways
with hope to cling to all that stays within
the hearts of mothers

Perry Douglas Sisk

Stolen Along Our Way

April 21, 2023

Let us take a trip now
and let us see how far we'll go
Do we start from where we are
or the beginning of this show
Going backward through some years
A time of lesser hate when folks just never
spoke of fate or leaving out
their fears
Folks would show a real concern
for neighbors moving in
take a dish of food prepared
a friendship hoped to win
With doors of homes that never lock
no fear of looking out
those days long past now taken back
one voice was left to shout
This journey all would recall
would they themselves so take
returning to a time most knew
we once again must make
where in time we stop to find
one kindred heart so real
This trip we took down
memory road
those dreams of past we steal

One Roaming Spirits Flight
April 15, 2023

How often have we heard
time sure does fly on by
Nowadays as many will say
just as much for asking why
As a child those hours dragged on so slow
we feared there was no end
Later on those hearts we broke
were feared to never mend

Those hearts repaired with love
we shared forever at a time
A clock that strikes we fail to wind
will always loose its chime
Now at Mid age we search the stage
that act we once portrayed
that impatience we held so long ago
now shelved leaves us betrayed

Those days that took forever to pass
while in our youth did take for granted
companionships miss tho still resides
in memory oh so slanted
These days we spend alone inside our empty homes
will soon one day serve to justify
our spirits need for many will see still roaming
unseen or heard that soar toward the sky

Perry Douglas Sisk

A GIFTED DIRECTION

May 12, 2023

As for we herein abide
in God's written word
As evil influences do descend
at first or second or even a third
Let it be said as written in stone
so long we do attest
to be so not so fearful to
never lose sight of one best
Faith was spoken in scripture
many times, never to be afraid
of evil crossing lines
Looking back upon our youth
a past was so misguided
while looking ahead in truth
Most fail to see one-sided
I know that too in life
we are given gifts and talents to amaze
As stars that light the heavens
above upon which we will gaze
With purpose, we sing, we write, and paint
So, filled with one that looks between the rain
the rainbow growing faint
with all of what is certain
one trust put upon
these words our lord had
written leaves no one left alone
Driving down a road we once
called freedom, a signpost up
ahead that said to turn these
exits we won't need them
the once-blue sky turned gray
and dark and oh so gloomy

Simple care once filled the air
no longer there for you or me
A town once small
with many crossing streets
not one single-stop sign
with a church where no one meets
Some soon realized the exit they had taken
from God's highway of truth
Few had thought they had been forsaken
not know what they would lose
Inside a town square now vacant and empty
of persons simply walking
No conversations are being held
by two that were not talking
A silence here in this town
so held in fear to never question why
God's ten commandments were
taken away the people lost
sight what's wrong what's right
did all come about in just one day so dreaded
One exit I took and by mistake did I look
just where it was so headed
to see where it ended
with no one as kindred
I saw what I had lost
A lesson life teaches our
father always reaches out to
remind us of the cost
Those laws God had written
as here I AM, for me as
while I'm sittin'
No fear of this life
may soon to be ending with what
faith and redemption sees
My one true Lord
with life everlasting
where I hope to be

Perry Douglas Sisk

These words most fail to mention

January 2024

Some have said it before
many will say it again
From that one and only time of begining
There is only one thats been
Able to teach not always to preach
those paths that we should walk
while some will resist
and always persist
in harshness some did talk
So many thought that they knew well
at times as i did too
See purpose for all he spoke
Though too that class
like broken glass
in pain what words invoke
With darkened skies
amidst their cries
the anger they did stoke

There will be ones
that spoke in many tongues
never hearing whats been said
For that lack of understanding
and for all they were demanding
That day who's blood was shed
Never saw that cross he carried
up that hill
where all had tarried
saw not the blood he'd spill
All true justice that was failed
on that cross of which
was nailed

A Deeper Contemplation

our redemption he had shown
those last three words he'd spoken
His anger was then woken
he said that it was done

Perry Douglas Sisk

BUSTER

August 15, 2023

Recently these thoughts of a story
came to me, I hope to share this with
others so let's begin and see
Several years back I guess
a solid decade or more
A friend that I had known that
had a heart as an open door
He called me one day to
ask if I could come by
Said he had something for me
though I didn't as what or why
Even though Sam lived a
good two hours away
I got into my truck to
drive and visit the very next day
I drove up to his home
where he lived still with his mother
to always see to her needs
just as one should honor
I stepped onto his porch and
said how y'all been
he said Oh fine dandy and
asked come on in
I said a warm hello to his mother
in her chair, her hair was white as snow
though she never hinted a care
They both asked if I could do em a favor
I couldn't of course say no
could you take this old hound
dog and give him a proper home
I stepped off of their porch and they
had him tied up to a tree there in the yard
one look I took at this old hound

35

A Deeper Contemplation

a kinship hit me hard,
Well I opened the door to my truck
and up he jumped so fast
He got right in the seat his fear
it didn't last
Sam and his mother said
thank you for this deed
they knew that I would give
this dog had everything he'd need
At the time this old hound dog
carried no known name
He held a manner calm and antsy still
he was so tame
On our way, we went along
I stopped off for a bite, I bought him
a burger and some fries on the side
he seemed to be so happy his
tail a wagging and his mouth open wide
I guess one could say
we bonded then and there
these days moving into years
a friendship found so rare
A name that I had chosen was Buster just because
as all them basset hounds go ya know they have big paws
he had eleven years with me
the two of us abide
This dog became my best bud
that stayed right by my side
One day i saw my hound just feeling well
The Doctor called it cancer and had no more to tell
All this tore me apart as
I watched him in such pain
the day I had to put him down
my heartbreak was so plain
I hold his ashes closely by
while trying hard to sleep
I know tho he is in heaven
where God won't let him weep

Perry Douglas Sisk

Thought to address

March 27, 2023

How many times did we find ourselves
in positions we were never suited for
Later down the road as we paced and
walked the floor whether right or wrong
did we always choose to ignore
At times speak aloud to
no one is there
just in hopes of drawing one near
or see someone with care
Only conveying thoughts that show
spirits low with one invading fear
no one hears our heavy sigh
let alone we'd shed one tear

We all go through those times being down
I guess we all can say
feeling tired weak or barely
willing to speak be it night or even day
This fear of knowing what others may think
of our display of expression
while they themselves bare times of despair
and so few would care to mention
Stranger though it is we finally
find the rudder that guide
our ships to peace
even if the process of ever
seeing progress given time
will anguish cease